An Introduction to

Email Marketing and Strategy

- An EmailFin publication -

Adam Redding

Table of Contents

Introduction

Thank you for purchasing this email guide - you have taken the first step toward improving your email marketing strategy! This guide was crafted with one critical goal in mind: To help business owners, marketers, and entrepreneurs make more money from email.

The strategies in this guide are meant to be used as tools to grow your business. This is not a one size fits all approach. As a business owner and digital marketer, I know that every business is different. The following content will provide guiding principles that will allow you to think strategically and creatively about your particular business so you can maximize your ROI from email marketing.

Additionally, this guide will not tell you which email vendor to use, nor will it provide step by step instructions for setting up an email campaign, or running an A/B test. This is a strategy tool that will help you to think intelligently about how to email your customers.

This guide is broken into three sections:

- **Crafting a great email:** I know a lot of you want to improve your email creative. So let's start here.

- **Developing an email strategy**: I will provide tools that you can use to build an email cadence that will maximize customer engagement.

- **Understanding the metrics:** Data, data and more data. I will explain the basic metrics you need to understand. Then I will show you how to use the data to think strategically about your email marketing strategy.

Once you understand the strategies in each section, you will see dramatic improvements to your email metrics, customer engagement, and sales.

This guide is concise, powerful, and it will absolutely help you grow your business. The tools in this will help you think differently about email marketing. And as you'll find out, thinking differently is paramount to email success.

Why focus on email?

Email is an incredibly efficient marketing channel. Ask yourself this question: where do you spend most of your time? Reading email, surfing the internet, perusing social media, watching TV, spending time with your family, etc. Internet advertising – such as paid search, display advertising, content marketing – is expensive. For most small businesses and entrepreneurs, advertising on TV and radio is cost prohibitive. The work place, as we know it today, revolves around email. And if you have a customer's email address, you can market to that person for a fraction of the cost of other channels. Thus, it's incredibly important to get your strategy right, because once you do, you can start counting the dollars.

How to use this guide

This guide should be used in two primary ways:

1. **A project plan tool** that will allow you to create an email strategy. I recommend that you go in chronological order. In each section, I provide tools and next steps that will guide you through crafting a strategy. If you take the time and follow the suggestions in each section, you will get the most value out of this guide. I expect that it will take you 4 – 5 hours to build a framework for your email strategy.

2. **A reference guide** that can be used when building an email, thinking about crafting a subject line, answering a question about email metrics, or anything mentioned in the following pages. Every time you build an email you can use this guide to make sure you've created an optimized email, as well as analyzed the metrics correctly.

Brief primer in email metrics

In section 3, I provide a full breakdown of email metrics that will give you the necessary foundation to think strategically about email marketing. However, in order to get the most value out of the first two sections, it's critical that you first understand the 'core' email metrics. Your email vendor houses all of this information so it should be easy to find. The following definitions and metrics will be referenced throughout the entire guide. Please skip to Section 3 if you want further explanation.

Delivered: How many emails were delivered. Inevitably some people enter bogus email addresses.

Unique Opens: The number of unique individuals who opened the email.

Unique Clicks: The number of unique individuals who clicked on the email.

Unsubscribes: The number of unique individuals who unsubscribed from your email distribution list, as a result of that specific email send.

Open Rate: Unique opens/Delivered. Allows you to understand what percentage of your customers opened the email. We typically look at 'delivered' (as opposed to the full email list) because it's a more accurate picture of how effective your subject line is.

Click to delivered rate (click through rate): Unique Clicks/Delivered. This is the traditional email barometer of success. This metric allows you to understand how many people clicked on your email, as a percentage of individuals that received your email. Your goal as an email marketer is to improve click through rates.

Unsubscribe rate: Unsubscribes/Delivered. This allows you to track how many people are actively opting out of your email list. You want to keep this rate as low as possible.

For example:

10,000 Delivered emails

2,000 Unique opens

300 Unique clicks

100 Unsubscribes

Open rate = 2,000 / 10,000 = 20%

Click through rate = 300 / 10,000 = 3%

Unsubscribe rate = 100 / 10,000 = 1%

Lastly, I will show a number of examples in this guide. You can always find more examples in the tips section at emailfin.com.

OK – We're ready to get started. Let's do this!

Section 1: Crafting a great email

Developing an email creative sounds simple, but before we dive in, let's define the basic terms used in email marketing. These concepts will be the foundation of understanding the topics in this guide.

- **Subject line:** This is the title of the email.

- **Email sender:** This is the address of the company or person sending the email.

- **Email creative:** This is the design of the email. It includes the format, the imagery, the content, the links, the disclaimers, and the CTAs.

- **Call to action (CTA):** These are the links that the email recipients click on. They are typically housed in a colored textbox so that customers can easily find where to click.

- **Headline:** This is typically the lead text in an email.

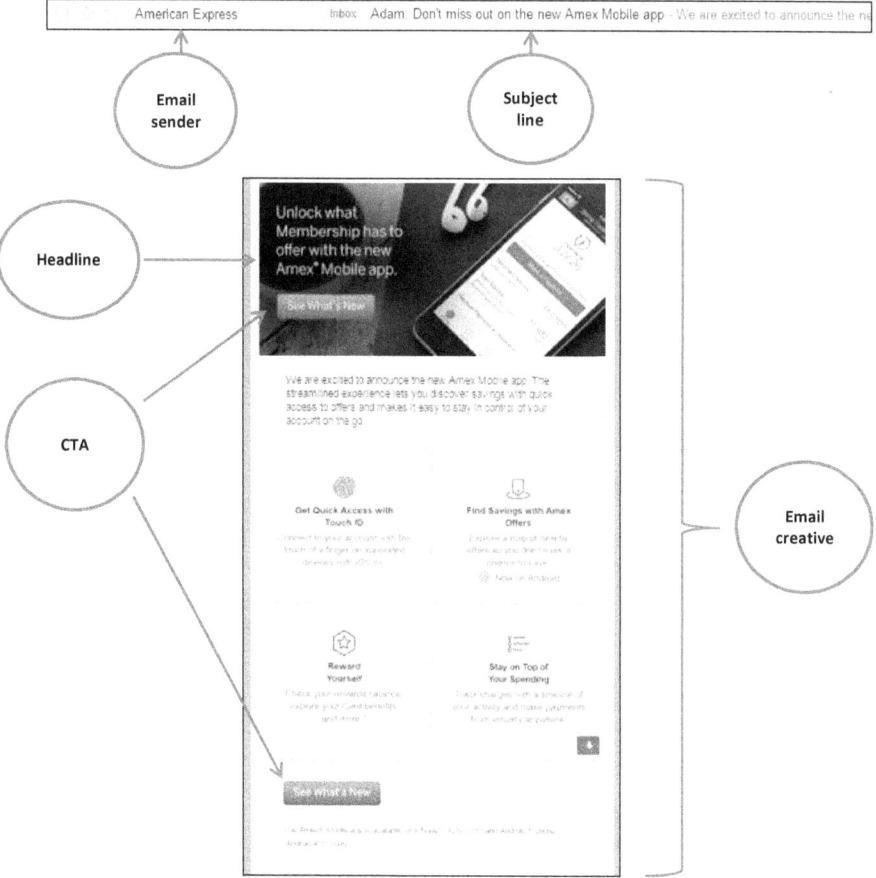

Now that you know the terms, let's talk about how to think about creating an email. Start by asking yourself the following questions:

1. What's the goal of the email?

2. How will I communicate that goal via content and imagery?

3. What will be the call to action (CTA)?

4. Where will the customer be directed?

5. What will the subject line be?

6. What does the email sender address look like?

7. How long should the email be?

8. How will all the above mix together to create a great email?

In my experience building email strategies for fortune 100 companies, non-profits, small businesses, and startups, six simple principles will help you answer the above questions. These principles will help you deliver powerful emails that will encourage your customers to buy.

1. Consistently deliver value

2. Have clear, large CTAs

3. More space, less clutter

4. Image is worth a thousand words

5. Don't forget the subject line

6. Keep it simple and concise

Consistently deliver value

The key to keeping your consumers engaged is consistently delivering value. But not just value – value that is new, novel and different from your competition.

What do I mean when I say value? To paraphrase dictionary.com, 'Value' is defined as something useful. Value can be a coupon, a new product, a new location, an article, an opinion, etc. In order to keep the interest of your customers, you need to understand what type of value you can provide.

For example, let's say you're a book retailer. As an email marketer, your email creatives need to focus on what your customers care about, which of course, are books (note that I did not say **buying** books). Simple, right? Here are examples of what a customer who purchases books might value:

- Book coupons
- New releases
- Book reviews
- Relevant industry information (i.e. ebook vs. paper book trends)
- New authors
- Best sellers

As it relates to books, your customers are probably interested in many things. You, as the small business owner, need to become an expert in this area (you probably already are, so share your knowledge and passion!).

Each email should focus on one value proposition. Put that value in your subject line, and deliver on that subject line in your email creative. Your customers will begin to think of you as more than just a retailer; they will view you as a subject expert. Open rates and click through rates will rise. Unsubscribe rates will fall (Section 3 will explain these metrics).

Next step: Think about your products. Pick a top seller and do the following:

- Make a list of all the reasons why a customer would buy from you.

- Make a list of all the reasons why a customer cares about your product.

- Make a list of what else the customer would be interested in that's related to that product.

- Once this is done, aggregate the unique value propositions from your lists. This aggregate list will form your value proposition bank, from which you can build an email strategy.

Email Tip

Constantly offering discounts via email can be a bad strategy. Remember, there's a good chance your competitors are offering discounts. All it takes is a Google search to compare prices. As an email marketer, you want your emails to tell a story about your company, connecting many values together. If you only focus on discounts, you'll only compete on discounts. Value strategy allows you to separate yourself from price.

Clear, large CTAs

This is email marketing 101. You need to have a clear CTA (call to action) that the customer cannot miss, whether your customers are viewing the email on a mobile device, a tablet, or a desktop. I've seen incredible progress over the past few years with companies optimizing their CTA strategy. If you don't give your customer a clear place to click, then the value you provide is all for naught.

What makes a good CTA?

- *Size:* Big. All of the content you craft should lead to this CTA. Using our example, as a book retailer, if you're promoting a 10% discount, your CTA should say "Get your 10% discount code".

- *Length:* You can include up to 5 – 7 words in your CTA. Shorter is not always better. The most important thing to remember is your CTA needs to convey the action your customer needs to take to get your offer. Make it easy on your customers.

- *Content:* I define success as getting purchases (as opposed to clicks). It's OK to sacrifice clicks if you can get more people to buy your product. Be specific, concise, and if you have an offer, use it.
    - For example: "Get your exclusive 5% discount code" Or "Get your offer code"

- *Color:* There's a lot of research on color selection. Red means stop, blue implies trust, green means go. In my experience, the most important fact when selecting a color is how that color interacts with your brand coloring. If red is the primary color of your website, then go with red. When your customer thinks about your brand, there will be an image. Make sure the color is consistent.

- *A/B testing:* You must always be testing! If you're not testing your CTA, then start right now. One simple way of testing without sophisticated software is to divide your email list into two equal, randomly selected groups. When testing, make sure to test only one item in the email (such as the CTA). Everything else should be consistent so that you can isolate your test. This will be discussed further in my next email guide, coming soon.

- *Number of CTAs:* More is not necessarily better. Some experts say you should have 2, 3 or even more CTAs in an email. My suggestion is a maximum of 2 CTAs, both related to the primary value proposition. If you're a book retailer and also sell videos, then at the bottom you can have a small CTA that says "Looking for discounts on videos? Click here." This should be a text link so that it doesn't distract from the primary CTA.

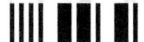

Example:

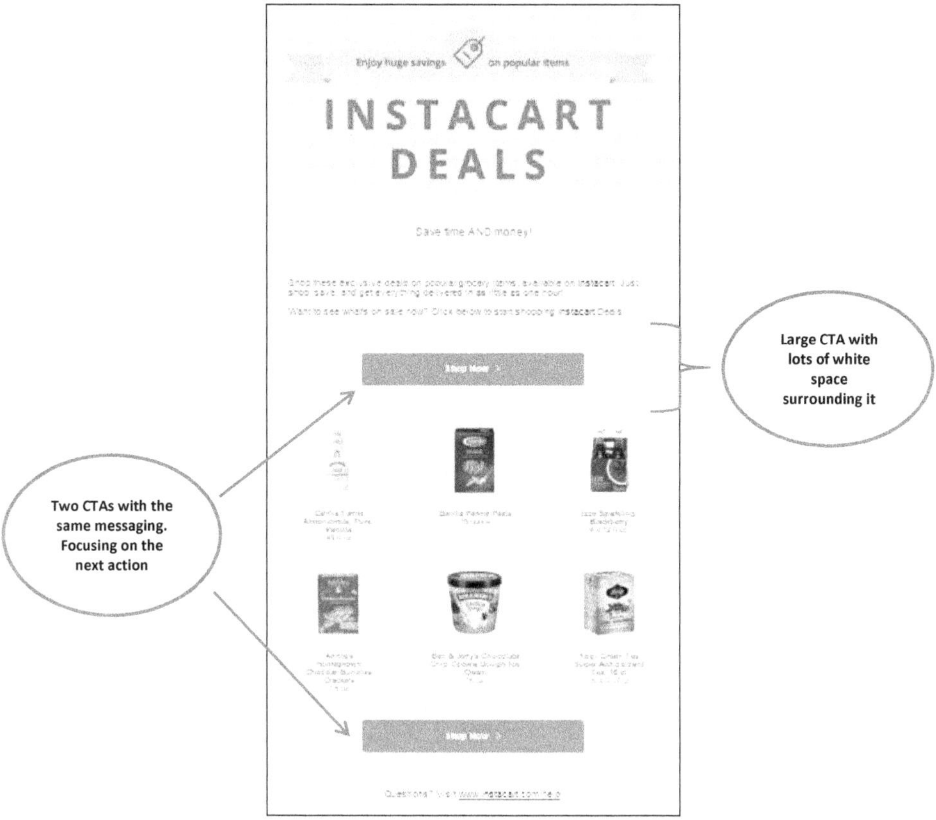
Enjoy huge savings
on popular items
INSTACART
DEALS
Large CTA with lots of white space surrounding it
Two CTAs with the same messaging. Focusing on the next action

Next step: Using the value proposition bank you just compiled, create a list of 10 CTAs that convey the actions you want your customer to take in less than 7 words.

More space, less clutter

Designing the creative is not easy. I strongly recommend that you use either a template that has the characteristics I describe next, or that you hire a designer to follow the below guidelines. Quality design is paramount to the success of your email. A few hundred dollars on a good web designer can easily turn a positive ROI.

- *North to south flow:* Depending on your customer base, more than 50% of email opens come from a mobile device. Your email should have a north to south flow, so your customers can easily scroll to see your content. Additionally, your content should be centered.

- *Spacing:*
  - The image and content should be separated by lots of space.
  - The CTA should have plenty of white space so that it is naturally separate from the rest of the email. This highlights the CTA, which makes it easy for your eye to find.
  - If you feel compelled to have more than one value proposition in your email, then it's important to have 'sectioning' in your email. This means your email should be broken into sections, so that it's easy for your eye to differentiate between offerings. I recommend using a light gray line to separate each section.

- *Content:* Your content should have a headline that clearly articulates what you're trying to convey. Ideally you can articulate your value proposition in 1 -2 sentences. This will occur in the body of the email. A great email uses the content to supplement the value delivered in the image. Remember, less is better.

- *Mobile optimized:* Your emails need to be optimized for mobile, per the above. If your emails aren't rendering correctly on mobile, take a look at your email metrics for desktop vs. mobile. The click through rates for desktop are likely dramatically higher.

Example:

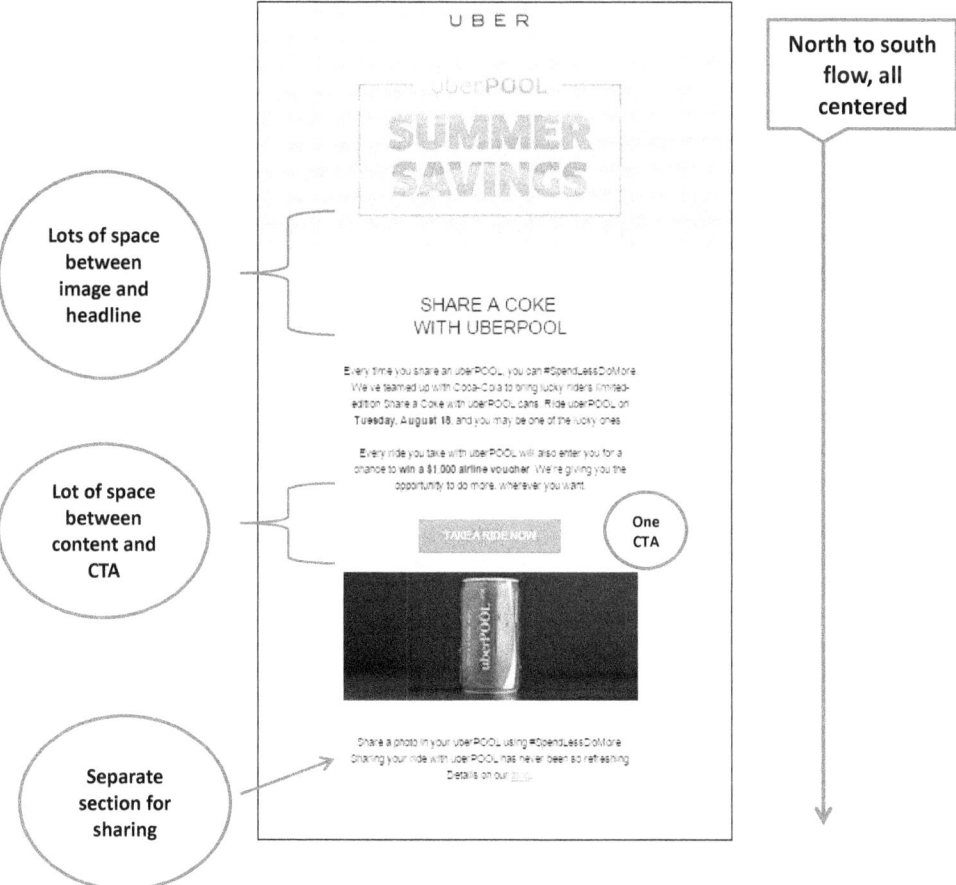

North to south flow, all centered

Lots of space between image and headline

Lot of space between content and CTA

One CTA

Separate section for sharing

Next step: Go to your inbox and find three emails that you absolutely love. Look at the design and ask yourself why they're so compelling. Write down the spacing and design aspects, and see what overlaps with the above.

Image is worth a thousand words

This is my favorite tactic in creating a great email. This one took me much longer to discover than it should have. I used to spend loads of time trying to perfect the email content. When I started testing images, I realized that it was easier to improve click through rate by changing the image than by changing content. Here's what you need to know:

- Images should be relevant to your customer base. If your primary customers are families, then the photo should have families engaging with your product.

- If the image is a stock photo, it should have people. This sounds obvious but adding people makes your email relatable.

- If possible, images should be designed, not pulled from stock photos. When you have an image designed, you can be much more creative in how it matches your email creative. Most companies use stock images. Remember, you need to be different. This also goes for social media marketing. I've consistently found that designed images are much more powerful than stock photos (if everyone starts using designed images, this may change).

- Images can have text: Your customers are going to look at your image. Make sure that your image conveys what you want them to know. Add a CTA or content to the image if you like, but above all, be sure to keep it simple.

Examples:

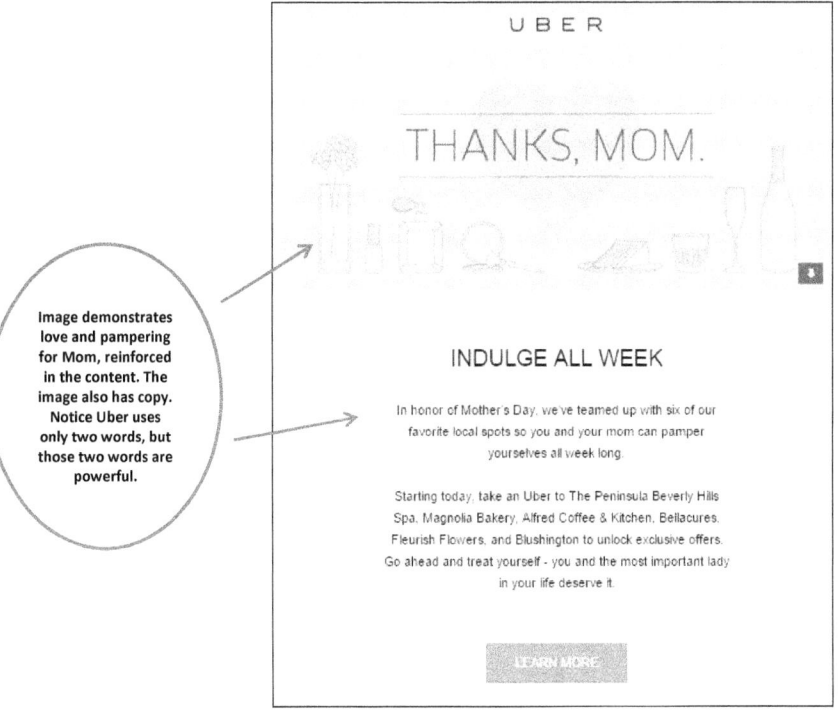

Image demonstrates love and pampering for Mom, reinforced in the content. The image also has copy. Notice Uber uses only two words, but those two words are powerful.

UBER

THANKS, MOM.

INDULGE ALL WEEK

In honor of Mother's Day, we've teamed up with six of our favorite local spots so you and your mom can pamper yourselves all week long.

Starting today, take an Uber to The Peninsula Beverly Hills Spa, Magnolia Bakery, Alfred Coffee & Kitchen, Bellacures, Fleurish Flowers, and Blushington to unlock exclusive offers. Go ahead and treat yourself - you and the most important lady in your life deserve it.

LEARN MORE

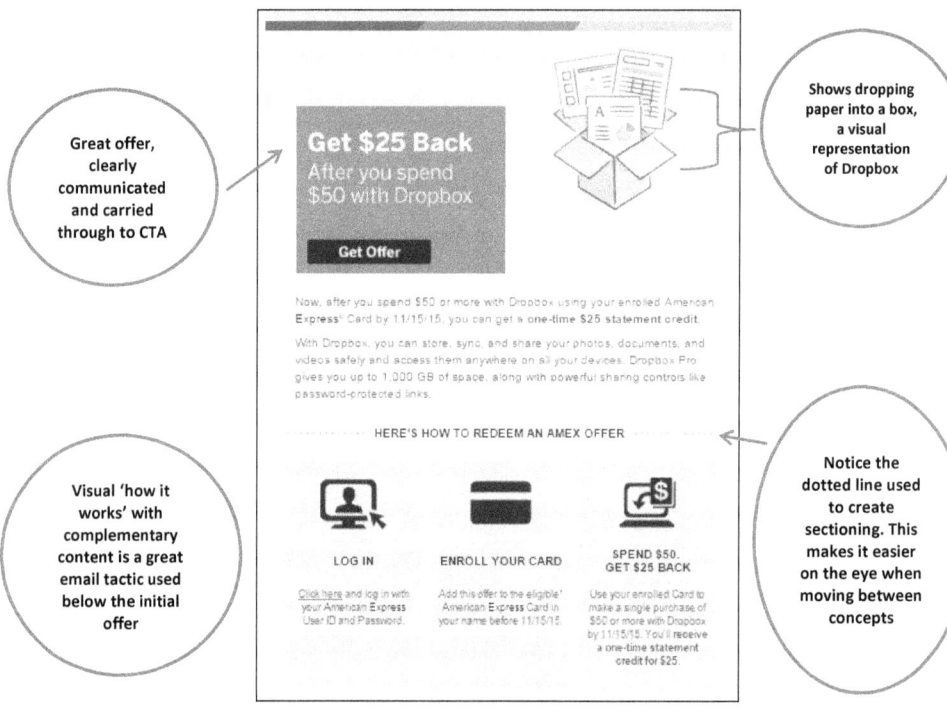

Next step: Brainstorm how you can represent your brand through an image. Answer the below questions:

- Is there a way to connect your product to the price visually?

- Pull up the list of value propositions from earlier. Are there images that represent each of these value propositions?

Don't forget the subject line

The subject line is your billboard. People will glance at it, and if something catches their eye, they'll do a double take (and maybe take an action!). It's easy to spend hours developing an email creative, then slot in a subject line with little thought at the last minute. I encourage you to think about both the creative and subject line before beginning development on the creative so that they are aligned. Here are a few tactics to use when trying to craft a great subject line:

- **Questions increase open rate**: I've found consistently that questions entice more people to open the email, with improvements in the range of 0 – 10%. Questions don't always lead to more clicks, but they are worth testing.

- **Numbers at the start of a subject line catch attention.** This can improve open rates from 0 – 5%.

- **Highlight an offer:** This works well, but don't overdo it. If every email highlights an offer, then your customers will stop opening.

- **Personalize the subject line:** "Dan, get great deals on new book releases." This can improve open rates from 0 – 5%.

- **Seasonal:** Seasonal subject lines work, but don't expect to see large increases vs. the average. Make sure to match the seasonal subject line with a seasonal creative, or your click through rate will decline (set expectations and fail to deliver). You can expect open rate improvements from 0 – 10%, but you might find a fall in click through rates.

- **Membership:** If you have a membership organization, speak to the benefits of that membership in the subject line. For example 'Membership benefit: $25 off your next TV'.

- **Think differently:** As I've discussed, and will continue to emphasize, different is always better in email. New products, new promotions, monthly summaries, asking for feedback – different approaches will keep your customers engaged. The above tactics can improve click through rate incrementally, but for step function improvements, new product launches are key.

Next step: Using the above principles, put together three subject lines that relate directly to three value propositions.

Keep it simple and concise

Per the name of the title of this section, I'll keep it simple. You have probably heard of KISS, keep it simple stupid. Emails should focus on one message. This message should be consistently conveyed in the subject line, image, content, and CTA. Your customers have very little time so get your point across quickly.

Example:

Subject line: We woke up like this

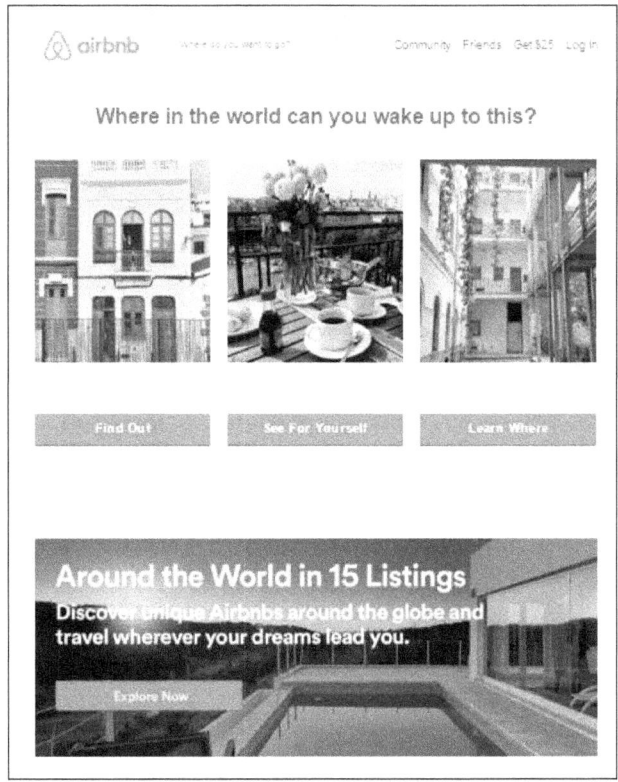

As you can see, there's almost no content in this email. The message is conveyed through images. This is an example of a Consumer Interest email, which I will describe in the next section.

Other email tactics that can help improve your email effectiveness

- *Animated GIFs*

- *Urgency marketing*: This is tactic is designed to create a sense of urgency by adding an end date to your offer. Make sure to follow up with the customer toward the end of the offer date.

- *Coupons*

- *Increase average order value:* You can offer extra dollars off if they purchase more. For example, get $50 off when you spend at least $100.

- *Scarcity:* This tactic relates to limited inventory. 'There are only 100 LED TVs available, so buy them fast.'

By now you have you have created a bank of value propositions, generated a list of CTAs, come up with a number of images that represent your value props, put together a few potential subject lines, and found some emails that are wonderfully designed. Lo and behold, you are well on your way to creating a great email. Now it's time to focus on building a strategy.

Section 2: Developing an email strategy

If you have already had a chance to implement some of the above tactics, hopefully you've had some success. In this section I'll introduce various tools that will allow you to build a success email strategy. Let's start with analyzing the competition.

What is my competition doing?

It's widely known that when SpaceX starting building rockets, they eschewed looking at the NASA designs so that their thinking wouldn't be anchored to NASA's school of thought. In doing so, SpaceX built rockets that were significantly more cost efficient.

Well good news: We're not building rocket ships! It's OK to look at what our competitors are doing. It's free insight, so let's take advantage of it.

I have summarized email strategies across industry leaders below. I have divided the emails into different categories. I recommend looking at every industry to gauge how best to start thinking about your business. I'll start first by describing the different types of emails your competition is sending out.

Email descriptions (examples are after the descriptions)

Product awareness: The goal of this email is to raise awareness of a particular product. For example, an email that describes what shoes are available at Bloomingdales.

Product reminder: The goal of this email is to re-engage the customer after he/she searched for a product. This is a form of retargeting. Retargeting is a tactic used to reengage customers based on their prior behavior. This will be further explained below.

Product interest: This is an email that provides interesting content related to a product. For example, a book retailer sends an email that describes the best fantasy books to read in your lifetime. This is engaging the customer with interesting content about a product that they might buy.

Deals: An email announcing a discount.

New Product: An email announcing the launch of a new product. For example, when UberRush launched, Uber sent an email announcing the launch of this new product feature.

Consumer interest: An email about a topic that your target customer might be interested. For books, this could be an email about up and coming authors. This is different from product interest because it is not directly related to the product, but is rather complementary to the product.

Feedback: An email requesting feedback on a customer experience.

New items (retailers): As it relates to retailers, an email announcing new retail items for sale. This is different from new products because new products relate to what you, as your company, are creating.

Order summary: An email detailing your transaction.

Rewards offer: An email describing how to earn rewards points.

Check-in: An email reminding you to check-in for a flight.

Get ready: An email giving you advice in anticipation of a customer experience. For example, an email reminding you of airline benefits before you fly that particular airline.

Ancillary product: An email promoting an ancillary product.

Payment reminder: An email reminding you of an upcoming payment.

Account snapshot: An email giving you a snapshot of your account.

Benefits reminder: An email reminding you of the benefits of your membership (for member based companies).

Social: An email alerting you to the action that a 'friend' has taken. Relevant if you have a social media sign up, such as sign up through Facebook, Google+, twitter, etc.

Bestselling: An email about the bestselling products.

Examples :

Product Awareness:

Promotion of available products at Bloomingdale's, with an emphasis on the latest items

Product Reminder:

A retargeting email based on the customer's online search behavior

amazon

Your Amazon.com Today's Deals See All Departments

Amazon.com has new recommendations for you based on items you purchased or told us you own

SPONSORED BY HAMILTON BEACH

Faster than a microwave - safer than a stovetop

› Shop now

Grove Square Hot Cocoa, Milk Chocolate, 24 Single Serve Cups
by Grove Square Hot Cocoa

Price: $8.91 ($0.37 / Count)
Subscribe & Save Price: $8.46 ($0.35 / Count)

At Grove Square we make delicious beverages that are compatible with your first generation Keurig K-Cup Brewer. The wonderful   Read More

Learn more   Add to Wish List

Eight O'Clock Coffee The Original, Keurig K-Cups, 72 Count
by Eight O'Clock Coffee

Price: $38.97 ($0.54 / Count)
Subscribe & Save Price: $37.02 ($0.51 / Count)

VARIETY DESCRIPTION: Our oldest recipe and most comp roast. Medium roasted to deliver sweet and fruity notes with a   Read More

Learn more   Add to Wish List

Green Mountain Coffee Breakfast Blend, Keurig K-Cups, 72 Count
by Green Mountain Coffee

Price: $39.96 ($0.56 / Count)

VARIETY DESCRIPTION: Balanced, sweet and inviting, Breakfast Blend is one of our most popular blends. Bright, sweet and   Read More

Learn more   Add to Wish List

27

Deals:

An image conveying the fall season, reinforced with copy

A clear discount

New Product:

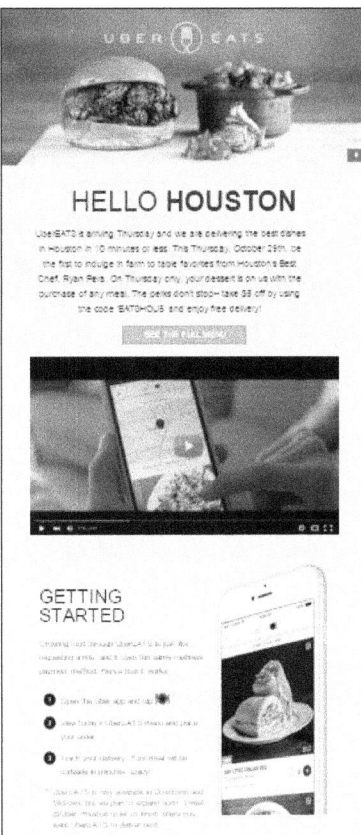

'How it works' video – This probably enhances click through rate (to be discussed)

A 'how it works' section is a great tool for new product emails, especially if using the product requires explanation

Consumer Interest:

Glassdoor wants you to search job postings and post reviews. An email about job interviews is a great way to pique interest

The CTA is relatively harmless. 'Read more' sounds enticing, without being overly salesy

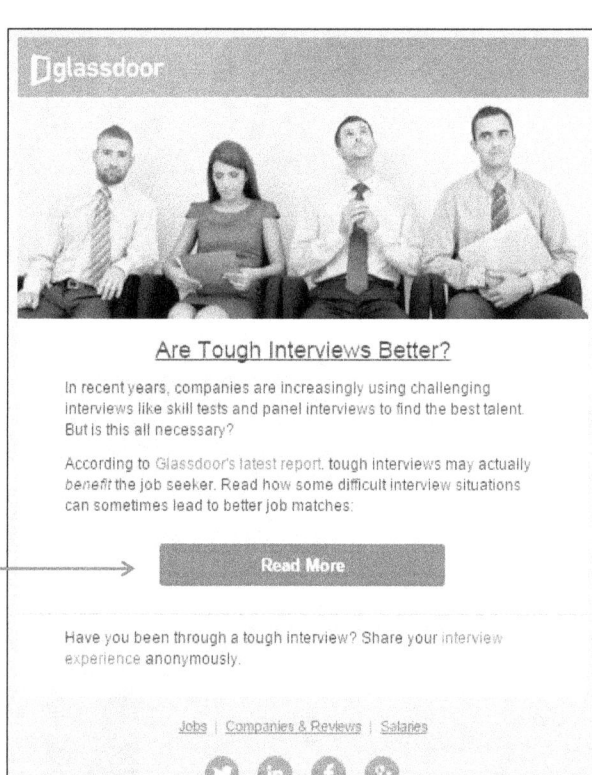

Are Tough Interviews Better?

In recent years, companies are increasingly using challenging interviews like skill tests and panel interviews to find the best talent. But is this all necessary?

According to Glassdoor's latest report, tough interviews may actually *benefit* the job seeker. Read how some difficult interview situations can sometimes lead to better job matches:

Read More

Have you been through a tough interview? Share your interview experience anonymously.

Jobs | Companies & Reviews | Salaries

Feedback:

The feedback email is a great tool for customer retention. You give your customers a safe forum to provide feedback. You can even put an offer here. Get 1,000 miles for telling us your thoughts

Simple CTA that is non-committal. The personal touch most likely improves click through rate

UNITED

We'd like to hear about your recent trip with United

It was a pleasure to serve you on your recent flight from Los Angeles to Houston. We are committed to earning your satisfaction by delivering a flyer-friendly experience every time you travel with us.

Please take a moment to let us know how we're doing by taking our brief survey. Your feedback will help us improve how we serve you and all of our customers.

We recognize that you have choices when you travel, and we thank you again for flying with us.

Continue >>

Sincerely,

Sandra Pineau-Boddison
Senior Vice President, Customers
United Airlines

31

New Items:

By listing out the new items, you are giving your customers something they have not seen before, which should entice click throughs. I would however recommend promoting fewer items

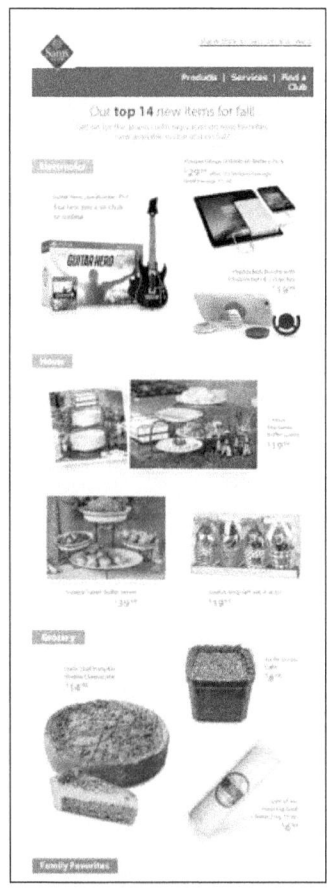

Ancillary Product:

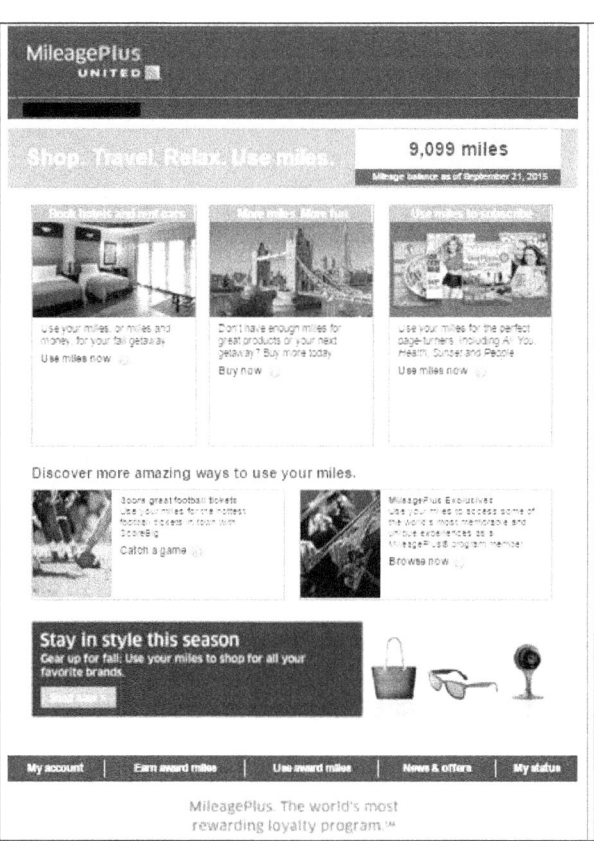

United Airlines is heavily promoting reward usage for other airline products, such as hotels or rental cars. These are of course directly related to flying.

Best Sellers

A best seller email uses social proof to entice engagement. By seeing what other people are purchasing, you're more likely to engage. Groupon is great at this.

Industry summaries:

Airlines

Frequency per month

Company	Product Awareness	Deals	Consumer Interest	Feedback	Rewards offer	Statement	Check-in	Get Ready	Ancillary Product	Total
Airline 1	3	3	0	1	3	1	Depends	Depends	0	11
Airline 2	3	1	1	1	2	1	Depends	Depends	1	10
Average	3	2	0.5	1	2.5	1	Depends	Depends	0.5	10.5

Banking/Credit

Frequency per month

Company	Payment Reminder	Product Interest	Product Awareness	New Product	Consumer Interest	Account Snapshot	Statement	Auto Pay	Payment Processed	Benefits Reminder	Total
Bank/CC 1	1	1	7	0	1	4	1	1	1	0	17
Bank/CC 2	1	1	1	1	0	0	0	0	1	1	6
Average	1	1	4	0.5	0.5	2	0.5	0.5	1	0.5	11.5

Clothing Retail Companies

Frequency per month

Company	Product Awareness	Deals	Consumer Interest	Rewards	Best Selling	Total
Clothing 1	8	24	2	0	0	34
Clothing 2	14	9	1	2	1	27
Average	11.0	16.5	1.5	1.0	0.5	30.5

Internet Company

Frequency per month

Company	Product Awareness	Consumer Interest	New Items	Social	Total
Internet 1	8	4	11	0	11
Internet 2	0	1	1	6	10
Average	4	2.5	6	3	10.5

Retail Companies

Frequency per month

Company	Product Reminder	Product Interest	Feedback	Product Awareness	Deals	New Product	Consumer Interest	Feedback	New Items	Order Summary	Total
Retail 1	2	2	1	1	0-1	0-1	0-1	0	Depends		7-8
Retail 2	0	0	0	16	0	0	0	0	0	0	16
Wholesale 1	0	2	9	2	0	0	0	1	0	0	14
Wholesale 2	0	0	11	6	0	1	0	1	0	0	19
Average	1	1	5	6	0	0	0	1	0		16

A few thoughts:

- The average company emails ~15x per month, or every other day. It varies by industry, so it's critical to take your purchase lifecycle into account when building your email strategy (discussed next).

- Companies with 'every day' purchases, such as retailers, email with greater frequency, up to 2-3x other industries.

- Every industry sends out product awareness emails. It's crucial to make sure your customers are aware of your products (sounds obvious but you would be surprised).

- The majority of emails are product awareness and deals, so those need to be in your repertoire. That said, we also now have an idea of how to differentiate your email strategy from the industry norms.

Next steps:

- Using the categories above, spend 15 minutes analyzing your competition, using the above categories. You will then be able to understand the standard email strategy in your industry.

- Decide which of the email types above make sense for your business. Once you've done that, you've taken the first step toward building an email strategy.

Competition Tip

If you have not done so already, I highly recommend that you sign up for your competitors' emails so that you can monitor exactly what they're doing. This will not only give you insight into their email strategy, but will allow you to passively monitor new products that are rolled out. You will often uncover new email tactics. If your competitors start using new email tactics multiple times, that's a good sign that they're working.

Understanding the purchase lifecycle of your customer

In order to develop a highly effective email strategy, it's critical that you understand your customers buying habits. The Rule of Seven marketing principle states that your customers need to see your

product seven times before becoming fully aware of your offer. Therefore, it's critical that you get in front of your customers often. But how can you determine the right timing? Answering the below questions will help you formulate that strategy.

- What is the purchase lifecycle for your customers (time between purchases)?

- How many times does your customer buy your product in a given year?

- Do your products experience macro seasonality (i.e. are there more popular times of year to buy your product)?

- Do your products experience micro seasonality (i.e. are there more popular times of the month or more popular days of the week to buy your product)?

- What is the average price point of your product?

- What percentage of your customers are repeat email openers? Put another way, how many customer open multiple emails from you?

- What percentage of your customers are repeat purchasers?

- What percentage of your business is from repeat purchasers?

- Have you segmented your customers into different groups? For example, do you have a group of customers you consider 'loyal'? And a group of customers you consider 'non-loyal'? We will dive into this further in my next email guide.

Let's examine two types of purchases: A customer buying a car and a customer buying clothes.

Questions	Buying a car	Buying clothing
Purchase lifecyle	Once every 4 - 5 years	Once a month
How many purchases in year?	0 - 1	10 - 15
Macro seasonality?	Memorial day, Labor Day, December	Holidays, Black Friday, December
Micro seasonality?	End of month, weekend	Weekend
Average price point?	$30,000	$75
What % of customers are repeat openers?	30%	30%
What % of customers are repeat buyers?	15%	40%
What % of business from repeat buyers?	30%	80%
Have you segmented your customers?	Yes	No

Buying a car

Awareness strategy

The learnings from the above chart, which I describe below, will allow us to develop an awareness strategy. An awareness strategy does exactly what it implies, builds awareness for your products with relevant content. Let's see how the above helps us develop an awareness strategy.

If your customer buys a vehicle once every 4 years, I would strongly urge you to avoid using the retailer strategy of daily emails. Many customers will unsubscribe quickly, as they don't want to think about buying a vehicle every week. It is however important to stay in front of your customers on a regular basis. What's the right timing?

Let's analyze the answers. Your customers are buying primarily over big holidays. Thus it's absolutely critical to create awareness during those popular buying seasons where you have the best chance of catching somebody interested in your product. Your customers buy at the end of spring, beginning of summer, and at the end of the year. Given that seasonality, it makes sense to send awareness emails at least once per quarter. This email can describe your product, as well as present any relevant seasonal deals. It can be timed near a major buying season.

Email #1: A quarterly product awareness email.

The next question is about micro seasonality. As we answered in the question bank, the most popular time of the month to buy a vehicle is at the end of the month, typically on the weekend. A reasonable conclusion from that data would be to send a monthly email, possibly toward the end of the month since that's when a high percentage of your customers will be purchasing. Furthermore, given that your customers tend to purchase on a weekend, you can send your email right before the final weekend (a Thursday or a Friday) of the month.

If you have a good idea of when that customer is purchasing, you should provide relevant and timely information about car buying to help them with their purchasing decision. For example, this could be an opportunity to discuss monthly car deals or to provide content on how to negotiate with a car dealership.

Email #2: A monthly email, delivered at the end of the month right before the weekend that provides content to help you make a smart buying decision.

Segmentation

I will now introduce the concept of segmentation. Segmenting separates your customers into different groups based on a variety of factors, such as demographics, location, purchasing habits, etc. The goal of segmentation is to provide relevant and personalized content to your customers. If you have a customer that is purchasing a car and she has two teenagers, it doesn't make sense to send her an email about buying a car seat.

In the car buying example, we'll focus on purchasing habits, and break our customers into two segments: Repeat buyers and non-repeat buyers. 15% of customers are repeat purchasers. If they're repeat purchasers, there's a good chance they are also brand loyalists. A brand loyalist, as it might imply, is somebody who has an emotional connection to your brand. Put another way, they love your product. If we connect this segmentation to email marketing, we could target the repeat buyer segment with monthly content that would be of interest to them. For example, you can provide content about new models or vehicle reviews and ratings. Another good business practice would be to provide loyalty deals. As it relates to car buying, you can offer customers a gift card the next time they use your service to purchase a vehicle. This will hopefully entice the customer to use your service for their next car purchase. These offers should be exclusive to your repeat buyer segment.

Email #3: A monthly email that provides loyalty value and interesting car buying content to repeat purchasers. This is an example of a 'segmented' email.

Targeting

A targeting email uses customer behavior (both email behavior and website behavior) as a tool for targeting your customers with relevant content. This is different from segmentation, as segmentation focuses on characteristics of those customers. For example, if you open an email, that says something about you. You read a subject line and took an action. Thus you're using the customer's actions to provide relevant content to that customer.

The next set of questions will allow you to think critically and strategically about your customers. 30% of your customers open your email more than once (you can access that information through your email vendor). That is powerful information. If the customer has opened multiple emails about car buying, he or she has indicated significant interest in your product. You can reasonably conclude that they are in-market to buy a car, or will be soon. You should target these customers and send them relevant information that can help them make a car buying decision (especially information that can help them buy through you). This should be done on a monthly, or potentially on a biweekly, basis. (Ideally, this is done on a triggered basis, which will be discussed in more detail in my next guide).

Email #4: A monthly/biweekly email, providing valuable information related to buying a vehicle to in-market buyers.

OK let's summarize the strategy, visualizing it in a table:

Email Type	Month 1	Month 2	Month 3
Awareness	X		
Monthly deals	X	X	X
Target	X	X	X
Segment	X	X	X
Total	4	3	3

As you can see above, on average we're sending about 3 – 4 emails a month. This is significantly less than other industries. This of course mirrors a purchase lifecycle that is much less frequent than you would find in many other industries. Now let's look at a much faster purchase cycle.

As it relates to segmentation and targeting, these can be incredible tools for winning loyal customers. In my next guide, I will further discuss these two tactics. I will introduce more advanced concepts around segmentation, such as using up to 6 customer segments to provide relevant content to your customers. I will also introduce more targeting tactics that you can implement over time, such as trigger based emails. And of course, you can always check my blog for updates and examples.

Buying clothes

Awareness strategy

If your customers are buying clothes more than 1x per month, you will need to be in front of them often. What's the right timing?

Your customers buy during the weekend and during big holiday seasons where there might be sales. Because buying tends to pulsate toward the weekend, you should be connecting with your customers on Thursday or Friday, before they've tuned out for the weekend to hit the malls. Given this buying behavior, it's logical to send a product awareness email as well as a deals email before the weekend. These emails can describe your product as well as any relevant seasonal deals.

Email #1: A weekly email that will be delivered before the weekend describing product awareness and/or deals.

Segmentation

We know that 40% of your customers are repeat purchasers. Clearly, you have a strong following, and it is critical that you reward these customers as well as continue to deliver a compelling story about your company. You should segment your repeat buyer population and provide them with two types of content:

- *Brand story:* Relevant content about your product that tells a story. For example, if you donate a portion of your proceeds to charity, send an email about this to engage your customers. You can then send a separate email about the sustainability of your products. It's critical that your brand loyalists are actively engaging with your story. This strategy can also be used for your entire email population.

- *Loyalty deals:* Send them, either once a month or once a quarter (not too often or they will just wait for it) deals exclusively for being a great customer.

Email #2: A monthly 'brand story' email, as well as a loyalty email. These are examples of a 'segmented' email.

Targeting

Similar to car buying, 30% of your customers open your email more than once. This behavior indicates intent to purchase. You should segment that population and send them relevant information that can help them make a purchasing decision. I would suggest either an email about new clothing items or a deals focused email. These are two concepts that an in-market clothing buyer might find very interesting.

Email #3: A targeted email about new clothing items or deals sent to an in-market buyer.

OK let's summarize:

Email Type	Week 1	Week 2	Week 3	Week 4
Product awareness	X	X	X	X
Weekly deals		X		X
Brand story	X		X	
New products	X		X	
Loyalty deals				X
Total	3	2	3	3

As you can see above, on average we're sending about 10-11 emails per month. This is significantly less than what other clothing retailers are doing (1x per day). Email marketing every day, or even multiple times per day, will hurt open rates and click through rates, and increase unsubscribe rates. At many of these large companies, once you embark on an aggressive email strategy, it is often hard to stop. You become reliant on the daily conversions that lead to a steady, but likely slowly declining source of revenue. Thus, when you analyze your competition, don't forget to think critically about why they might be implementing a certain email strategy.

Next steps

- Answer the above questions, ideally creating a table similar to the one above.

- Commit to three types of emails and plot them on a calendar.

Common email strategies

So far, I've showed you how to analyze what your competition is doing, in an effort to establish a baseline of what's happening in the marketplace. Then, using the customer purchase process as a guide, I walked you through how to create a core email strategy. Finally, I'm going to share with you some successful supplementary email strategies that you can add to your final work plan.

1. **Welcome email:** According to ometria.com, welcome emails generate 4x the open rates and 5x the click rates of other promotional emails. If somebody is new to your product, it's a great opportunity to introduce them to your product. The open rates for welcome emails can be as high as 70%.

2. **New customer email series:** Now that you have identified a new customer, you can present them a series of emails introducing your brand. This can include information describing your brand and why your company is awesome, reminder emails about your product (when it will arrive, features of the product, best practices, etc.), as well promotions for ancillary products. 'Hey you who just bought a crib, how about a car seat as well?'

3. **Abandon Cart:** According to Baymard Institute, an independent web research company in the UK, 67% of online shopping carts are abandoned. If you're an ecommerce company, and consumers are leaving your cart, it's critical that you retarget them. This information should be readily accessible through your website analytics tool. This same concept can be used if you're a lead generation company. You can send customers who have abandoned their carts a reminder email in which you provide a value proposition, such as a coupon, or a compelling reason why they should finish the process.

4. **Social emails:** With Instagram, Facebook, Twitter, Pinterest, Snapchat, Periscope, and God knows what else, it's critical to engage your customers in social channels. You should always include the social icons at the bottom of your email. If customers need to sign up to use your program, then use Facebook login. This allows you to send 'social' emails, which allow your customers to see how their friends are engaging with your product. This can be a very powerful tool to increase your email engagement and can differentiate you from your competition.

5. **Ecommerce receipts:** According to receiptful.com, email receipts get an average open rate of 70.9%. If somebody just purchased a product, they are waiting to get a receipt. So give them what they want! And by the way, use it to promote ancillary products, or to tell your brand story. I strongly suggest offering up a 'Thank you' as well. Good manners do not go unrecognized!

Bringing it all together

It's time to finalize the email strategy into a project plan. I'll take you through both examples below.

Buying a car:

My initial email strategy is as follows:

Email Type	Month 1	Month 2	Month 3
Awareness	X		
Monthly deals	X	X	X
Target	X	X	X
Segment	X	X	X
Total	4	3	3

Looking at some of the common email strategies I described above, it would make sense to have a welcome email. If somebody signs up for my email list, I should introduce them to my website and let them know how to buy from me.

Additionally, once they buy from me, I should send them a 'Thank you' email. After making a purchase, you often get so involved in the action of buying a product (especially an offline purchase) that you forget about your online experience. Thus a thank you email is a perfect way to reengage that customer after they have used your product. This would also be a good place to introduce a feedback email. I like to separate the two because feedback is incredibly important to enhancing your business, so in my opinion, it's worth it to have a dedicated feedback email.

Lastly, I've decided to not include a new customer email series, social emails, or abandon carts. For this industry, because the purchase doesn't happen often, I don't feel at launch I need a new customer email series. As it relates to social emails, social engagement is usually more impactful with purchases that have higher frequency. Lastly, I can add an abandon cart email in the future. As I previously mentioned, I will discuss targeting and segmenting in more detail in my next strategy guide.

Email additions: Welcome, Thank you, Feedback

Email Type	Month 1	Month 2	Month 3
Awareness	X		
Monthly deals	X	X	X
Target	X	X	X
Segment	X	X	X
Welcome	X		
Thank you			X
Feedback			X
Total	5	3	5

We're actively engaging our customer base with relevant emails, but because this purchase doesn't happen often, we're emailing significantly less (4-5x month) than the 15x per month we see across the board.

Buying clothes

Similar to car buying, I'm going to add a Welcome, Thank you and Feedback email. Because you can buy your clothes online, I'm going to replace the Thank You email with a Receipt email, as it's more contextually relevant for clothing, as well as more likely to have a higher open rate. You can include similar content in the receipt email as well. In addition, I will include an abandon cart email. Since clothing is such a high volume product, many consumers will spend a lot of time on your site thinking about purchasing. There's likely to be significant cross shopping with your competition, so it's critical to reengage your shoppers if they start adding clothes to their cart.

Lastly, given the fact that consumers love to show off their clothes with their friends, this is a product that has a high propensity for social engagement. By having your customers sign up through Facebook, you can take advantage of that. I would recommend setting a weekly or a biweekly cadence for social emails, as opposed to an email every time one of your customer's friends takes an action. This will reduce unsubscribes.

Email additions: Welcome, Receipt, Feedback, Abandon Cart, Social

Email Type	Week 1	Week 2	Week 3	Week 4
Product awareness	X	X	X	X
Weekly deals		X		X
Brand story	X		X	
New products	X		X	
Loyalty deals				X
Welcome	X			
Feedback			X	
Receipt		X		
Abandon Cart	X			
Social	X		X	
Total	6	4	5	3

We're emailing our customers about once every two days. We're not flooding our customers with deals or awareness emails. We're providing them relevant content, introducing them to our brand, and building brand loyalty through brand story emails, as well as social emails.

Section 3: Understanding the metrics

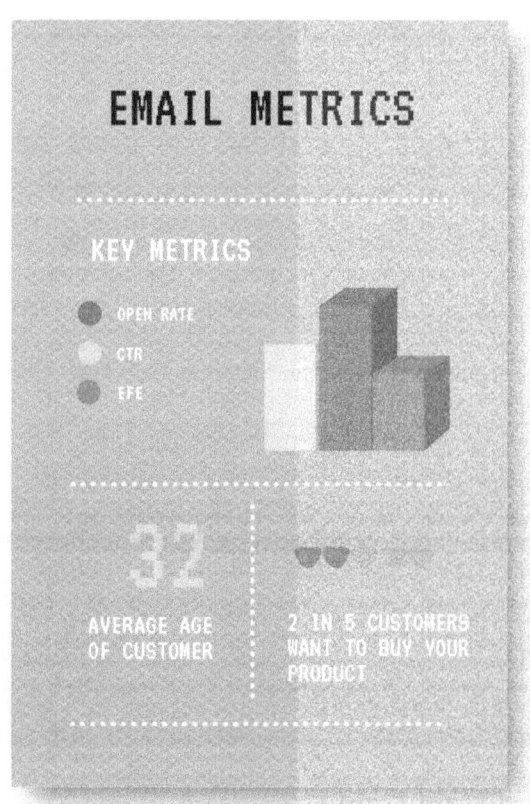

In order to earn your email marketing black belt, you need to understand the metrics. In my experience, I learned quickly that understanding the data was instrumental in building a successful email strategy. Not only should you be able to define each metric, but you should understand how to think about each metric critically and strategically. Data is your best friend. Sometimes it will make you unhappy, but remember, it's always there for you when you need it most.

An introduction to basic email analytics

The below email metrics are essential for creating a winning email strategy.

Email metrics bank:

Sends: Size of distribution list.

Delivered: How many emails were delivered. Inevitably some people enter bogus email addresses.

Opens: How many times the email was opened. This is the absolute number. So If John Stone opened the email twice that would count as 2.

Unique Opens: The number of unique individuals who opened the email.

Clicks: The number of times someone clicked on your CTA. Note, if John Stone clicked the email twice, that would be counted as 2 clicks.

Unique Clicks: The number of unique individuals who clicked on the email.

Unsubscribes: The number of unique individuals who unsubscribed from your email distribution list, as a result of that specific email send.

Unique Visitors: The number of unique individual who have engaged with your hosted web page.

Prospect: A unique individual who has taken an action to indicate interest (typically by submitting some combination of personal information).

Sale: A unique individual who has purchased your product.

My recommendation is to always focus on the 'unique' numbers. In my second edition, I'll get into advanced analytics that explains how to think about repeat behavior.

Now that we understand the key metrics, let's understand how to analyze them using an example.

Email analytics bank:

The metrics highlighted in blue are the most critical metrics to focus on.

Delivered rate = Delivered/Sends.

Open rate = Unique opens/Delivered.

Click to open rate = Unique clicks/Unique opens

Click to delivered rate (click through rate) = Unique clicks / Delivered

Unsubscribe rate = Unsubscribes / Delivered

Drop off rate = (Unique clicks - UVs on landing page) / Unique clicks

Conversion rate = Prospects / UVs

Close rate = Sales / Prospects

Funnel efficiency = Sales / UVs

Email funnel efficiency = Sales / Delivered

RPU = Revenue / unique visitors

RPD = Revenue / delivered email

*Blue indicates the most useful and heavily used email metrics

Analytics explained

Delivered Rate: Allows you to understand how many good email addresses you have. This should be above 95%.

Open Rate: Allows you to understand what percentage of your customers opened the email. We typically look at 'delivered' (as opposed to 'sends') because it's a more accurate picture of how effective your subject line is.

Click to open rate: This allows you to assess how well your email performed purely on click rate. Put another way, regardless of how your subject line performs, your click to open rate shows the success of your email content.

Click to delivered rate (click through rate): This is the traditional email barometer of success. This metric allows you to understand how many people clicked on your email, as a percentage of individuals that received your email. Your goal as an email marketer is to improve click through rates.

Unsubscribe rate: This allows you to track how many people are actively opting out of your content. You want to keep this rate as low as possible.

Drop off rate: This allows you to track how many people drop off before they hit your landing page. This is especially relevant if you have a login page. It's critical to understand how many customers do not login. This will also allow you to understand if there are load time issues or other technical issues at play.

Conversion rate: This tracks how many customers become prospects. You should always be maximizing this metric. Some businesses might not have the concept of a prospect, so you can skip this if that's the case.

Close rate: This metric tracks how many sales you were able to generate from your prospects. This is another area of optimization.

Funnel efficiency: This allows you to analyze the efficiency of your unique visitors. Independently of email, when you try to understand your website or mobile app business, it's critical that you understand how many unique visitors turn into sales.

Email funnel efficiency: This is a metric used to identify the success of an email. Ultimately, we want to understand how many customers purchased from a particular email. The exciting thing about this metric is once you understand what one email address is worth, you can conceptualize how many email addresses you need to meet your relevant business goals.

RPU: This is similar to funnel efficiency, but looks at revenue. Once you understand revenue per UV, you can begin to build other marketing strategies outside of email.

RPD: Similar to RPU, this allows you to understand how much each individual email is worth to your business.

Example: Walking through the metrics

Metric	Control Email 1
Email Addresses	10,000
Delivered	9,900
Opens	2,500
Unique Opens	2,000
Clicks	450
Unique Clicks	300
UV's	250
Prospects	30
Sales	10
Success Rate	99.00%
Unique Open Rate	20.20%
Unique Click to Open Rate	15.00%
Unique Click Through Rate	3.03%
Dropoff Rate	16.67%
Conversion Rate	12.00%
Close Rate	33.33%
FE	4.00%
EFE	0.10%

Let's dissect the above email.

- It was sent to 10,000 people. We had 100 bogus email addresses. Some customers will inevitably enter fake email addresses and phone numbers.

- The unique open rate was 20.2%. We'll never get a 100% open rate, so forget about it. Remember, somebody needs to open the email first. You can take a haircut to how many books you can sell by 80%.

- The click to open rate was 15%. Out of the 2,000 people that actually saw your email, 300 took an action. When thinking about this, the person really took three actions. He or she read a subject line, then read your email, then clicked. This customer should be considered in-market.

- The click through rate was ~3% (300/9,900). ~3% of the customers who received this email clicked on the CTA. Our goal as email marketers is to increase the click through rate.

- Drop-off Rate: Almost 17% of customers dropped off after they clicked. Depending on how consumers access your site, a 17% drop-off rate might be considered really good or really bad. If that number is higher than 25%, I would actively research what is happening. There might be a simple technical issue. If so, you just got back 25% of your email traffic!

- Email funnel efficiency (EFE): This is .1%. With 10,000 emails, you can sell 10 books. If you can get that up to 20,000 emails, you can sell 20 books without changing anything about the email. This metric is critical to understand scalability. Of course, not all customers are created equal, so how you acquire those email addresses is critical for scaling.

Now let's A/B test this email. An A/B test is when you change an element of the email in order to see if that element improves the performance (the metrics above) relative to an original version of the email (typically called the control). In order to run an A/B test, you want to test only one variable so that you can isolate and analyze whether that element had an impact to the performance metrics.

In the below example, we've run two tests vs. the control. The first test is changing the subject line (optimized subject line), and the second test is changing the content (optimized content). These are for explanatory purposes only.

Email Testing Example			
	Control	Optimized Subject Line	Optimized Content
Metric	*Email 1*	*Email 2*	*Email 3*
Email Addresses	10,000	10,000	10,000
Delivered	9,900	9,800	9,800
Opens	2,500	3,000	3,000
Unique Opens	2,000	2,750	2,750
Clicks	450	450	600
Unique Clicks	300	325	550
UV's	250	250	450
Prospects	30	35	50
Sales	10	11	15
Success Rate	99.00%	98.00%	98.00%
Unique Open Rate	20.20%	28.06%	28.06%
Unique Click to Open Rate	15.00%	11.82%	20.00%
Unique Click Through Rate	3.03%	3.32%	5.61%
Dropoff Rate	16.67%	23.08%	18.18%
Conversion Rate	12.00%	14.00%	11.11%
Close Rate	33.33%	31.43%	30.00%
FE	4.00%	4.40%	3.33%
EFE	0.10%	0.11%	0.15%

Email #2 vs. Email #1

After dissecting email #1, I looked at my Unique Open Rate (Uniques/Delivereds) and decided that 20.2% wasn't good enough. I split the 10,000 emails into two groups (for simplicity, I have kept the two test groups above at 10,000 email addresses so it's easy to understand the metrics. In practice, the two groups would consist of 5,000 emails each), and tested two different subject lines. The results are interesting:

- Open rate jumped up to 28%. That's 8 percentage points better, which is a performance improvement of 39% (you actually got 39% more people opening your email). Fantastic work, right?

- Unique click to open rate fell by over 3 percentage points, or 21%. It seems that while your subject line got more people opening your email, you lost many of those incremental opens because the content hadn't been optimized.

- Unique Click Through Rate: Overall, your click through rate jumped up to 3.32%, a 9% improvement. Click through rate is your email barometer, so this was a positive optimization, even though the Click to Open rate dropped. Now do you understand why it's important to distinguish between the two? They can tell you different stories.

- Overall, you sold one more book out of 10,000 emails, as your EFE went from .1% to .11%. Thus you improved how effective your emails are by 10%. Your key success metrics all improved:
  - o Unique Open rate: Increased 39%
  - o Unique CTR: Increased 9%
  - o EFE: Increased 10%

- For our next test, a logical optimization would be to improve our creative, as we've done a great job enticing more people to open the email.

Email #3 vs. Email #2

Since Email #2 was the winner, as determined by Open Rate, Unique Click Through Rate and EFE, email #2 now becomes your control. Let's see what happens when we try to optimize the creative.

	Control	Optimized Content
Metric	*Email 2*	*Email 3*
Email Addresses	10,000	10,000
Delivered	9,800	9,800
Opens	3,000	3,000
Unique Opens	2,750	2,750
Clicks	450	600
Unique Clicks	325	550
UV's	250	450
Prospects	35	50
Sales	11	15
Success Rate	98.00%	98.00%
Unique Open Rate	28.06%	28.06%
Unique Click to Open Rate	11.82%	20.00%
Unique Click Through Rate	3.32%	5.61%
Dropoff Rate	23.08%	18.18%
Conversion Rate	14.00%	11.11%
Close Rate	31.43%	30.00%
FE	4.40%	3.33%
EFE	0.11%	0.15%

- Open rate didn't change since we used the same subject line

- Unique Click to Open Rate jumped to 20%, representing a ~70% improvement in clicks. That's an outstanding result (and incredibly challenging to do in practice).

- Your click through rate is now 5.61%, which is a 69% improvement vs. email #2.

- Now that you have generated 69% more traffic to your website, you will naturally see a decline in conversion and close rate, which you see above. Because we've begun optimizing, we're probably getting a more users who might be less in-market. That's a good thing – they're interacting with your product and will hopefully come back to buy at a later date.

- Your EFE jumped to .15%, representing a 36% improvement vs. email #2, and a 50% improvement vs. email #1.

The two examples I outline above show powerful improvements using the concept of A/B testing. By understanding how to analyze the email metrics, you can determine which areas of the email you should optimize. In practice, when you start testing, there's a good chance you start seeing wins similar to what I described above. As you become a smarter email marketer, those improvements will become harder to find as you squeeze as much out of the funnel as you can. That's why it's critical that you continue to think differently about your content, so that you can continually surprise and wow your customers.

Lastly, you do not need a fancy email client to run A/B tests (they do of course help, and are highly recommended). All you need to do is separate your email population into two groups, ensuring that the selection is random. You need a statistically significant amount of email addressed to start identifying success and failure. In my experience, you can be confident of the results when you have about 1,000 email addresses, or two buckets of 500.

What do successful email metrics look like?

If you're new to email marketing, or even an experienced email marketer, you might be wondering - how do I compare to the competition? What is good and what is bad? I've created general ranges below. Each industry can be dramatically different and has a different type of customer base. Because of that, I have only included ranges below. I did not include conversion rate, close rate and funnel efficiency metrics below as they change dramatically depending on what product you're selling. Hopefully the below will be helpful for you as you think about your performance relative to what is possible.

If you send me your email metrics to emailfinblog@gmail.com, I will average, anonymize and post them on www.emailfin.com so we can get a clearer picture of email success and failure by industry.

Metric	Competitive Metrics
Success Rate	95 - 99%
Unique Open Rate	10 - 25%
Unique Click to Open Rate	5 - 10%
Unique Click Through Rate	1 - 3%
Drop-off Rate	0 - 10%
Drop-off Rate with login	30 - 50%

Conclusion

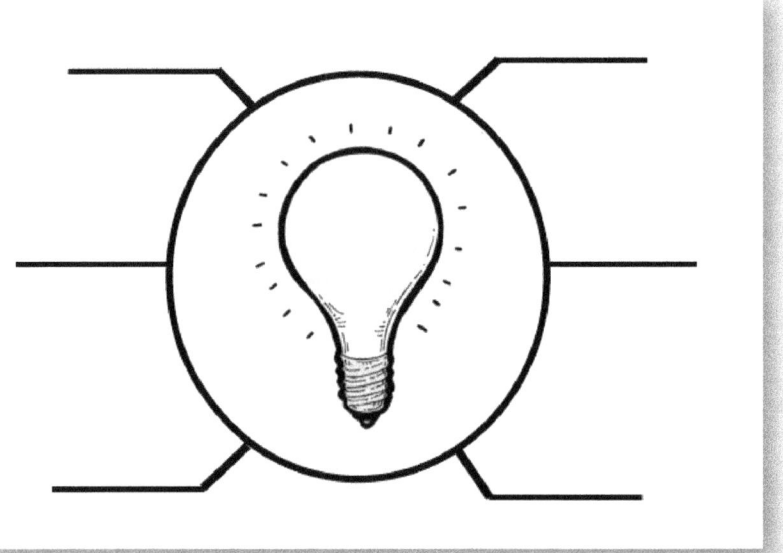

Conclusion

Hopefully you have found the information in this guide useful, and you're already seeing dramatic improvements to your email engagement, leads and sales. In Section 1, I introduced you to the six principles of developing an email creative. In Section 2, I outlined a strategy for developing an email marketing strategy. Lastly, in Section 3, I explained the key email metrics, what they mean, and how to think about them strategically.

If you have followed all the suggestions in this guide, you have done the following:

- Listed why a customer cares about your product and created a bank of value propositions as to why they would buy from you.

- Created 10 CTAs to test in emails.

- Identified spacing and design elements that you think will resonate with your customers.

- Discovered ways to represent your brand and your product benefits through imagery.

- Based on your value props, you have created at least three subject lines that you think will entice your customers to open your email.

- Analyzed your competition and plotted out their email marketing strategy.

- Generated a list of email types that you would like to add to your email strategy.

- Plotted out the emails into a calendar for deployment.

- Committed to sending three emails for testing.

Your next step is to take all of the above information and put it into a project plan, so that you can effectively manage your email marketing. I also strongly recommend adding all of your planned emails to an email calendar, so that you can visualize your strategy. Lastly, and this is possibly the most important item, you should create a spreadsheet where you can track your email performance. This will help you identify opportunities to optimize, as well as not forget the wins you have already had.

In my next edition, I will dive deeper into the analytics, such as going into more depth around the intersection between email analytics and website/mobile analytics. I will introduce the concept of lifecycle marketing, providing a framework to think about email marketing at different stages of the consumer experience. I will discuss more in-depth segmenting and targeting strategies that will turn you into an email wizard. I will also further discuss ancillary email strategies, such as new customer email series, e-commerce strategies, and membership strategies.

If you have any questions or want to provide any feedback, please email me at emailfinblog@gmail.com. I hope this guide has been useful and best of luck with your email marketing!

www.ingramcontent.com/pod-product-compliance
Lightning Source LLC
Chambersburg PA
CBHW061221180526
45170CB00003B/1097